USING

MW01504764

PRAYERS
THAT
WORK

KEVIN L A EWING

Prayers That Work
Using Scriptures That Bring Change

Kevin L.A. Ewing

For more information on Kevin L.A. Ewing please visit
www.kevinlaewing.com

Rights and Use Granted by I.P. Creator Kevin L. A. Ewing to
The Sign Me Agency LLC.

The Bible verses used came from the King James Version.

Printed in the United States of America First Edition

12345678910

TABLE OF CONTENTS

TABLE OF CONTENTS

TABLE OF CONTENTS

FOUNDATIONAL
PRAYERS

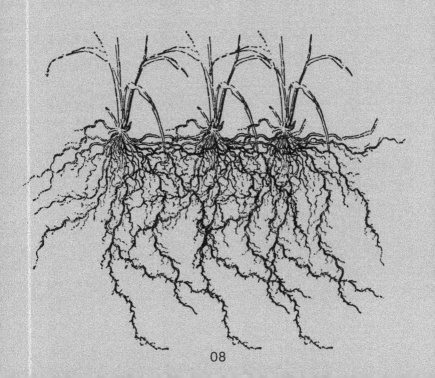

PRAYER OF SALVATION

Dear God, I believe that You sent Your only begotten Son Jesus Christ, to die on the cross, so that by believing in Him I can be forgiven of my sins and be redeemed because His innocent blood was shed for me. I believe that it is only through His death on the cross and resurrection that I can be made right with You.

I confess Lord that I am a sinner and in need of a Savior. I believe that Jesus Christ was the sinless sacrifice that died to pay the price for my sins and I believe that He is the only person who is qualified to die for me, for He alone lived a sinless life and died as an innocent victim.

Thank You for loving me enough to send Your only begotten, sinless Son to become a Man, so that He could offer Himself as the perfect Lamb of God, Who takes away the sins of the world. Thank You for loving me and dying for me. Help me to live a life that honors You, in thought, word and deed.

Father, I repent of all my sins and I turn away from them to Christ. I pray that You would keep me holy and set apart for You as I seek to live for You. I ask this in the name of Jesus Christ, my Savior. Amen.

PRAYER OF REPENTANCE

Heavenly Father, You know the depths of my sorrow over my sin. Even though it's painful, I know this sorrow is a gift of grace. I would far rather be aware of my sin and mourning over it, than to be oblivious of it and self-satisfied because awareness of it is the first step towards confessing it, repenting of it, forsaking it, and turning back toward You. I thank You for granting me a fresh awareness of my sin before You Oh Holy God! Not so I can wallow or berate myself, but so I can come to the cross for cleansing.

Father, Psalm 51:1-18 says, "Have mercy on me, O God, according to Your steadfast love; according to Your abundant mercy blot out my transgressions. Wash me thoroughly from my iniquity, and cleanse me from my sin! For I know my transgressions, and my sin is ever before me. Against You, You only, have I sinned and done what is evil in Your sight, so that You may be justified in Your words and blameless in Your judgment.

Behold, I was brought forth in iniquity, and in sin did my mother conceive me. Behold, You delight in truth in the inward being, and You teach me wisdom in the secret heart.
Purge me with hyssop, and I shall be clean; wash me, and I shall be whiter than snow.

11

PRAYER OF REPENTANCE

Let me hear joy and gladness; let the bones that You have broken rejoice. Hide Your face from my sins, and blot out all my iniquities. Create in me a clean heart, O God, and renew a right spirit within me. Cast me not away from Your presence, and take not Your Holy Spirit from me.

Restore to me the joy of Your salvation, and uphold me with a willing spirit. Then I will teach transgressors Your ways, and sinners will return to You. Deliver me from blood guiltiness, O God, O God of my salvation, and my tongue will sing aloud of Your righteousness. O Lord, open my lips, and my mouth will declare Your praise.

For You will not delight in sacrifice, or I would give it; You will not be pleased with a burnt offering. The sacrifices of God are a broken spirit; a broken and contrite heart, O God, You will not despise. Do good to Zion in Your good pleasure; build up the walls of Jerusalem; then will You delight in right sacrifices, in burnt offerings and whole burnt offerings; then bulls will be offered on Your altar."

Father, having believed Your promises, I receive Your forgiveness. I recognize that You remove my sins as far as the east is from the west, choosing to remember it no more according to Psalm 103:12. There are no words to thank You for this grace. It's in the name Jesus, my Savior and Lord, I pray. Amen.

MY HEART AND FORGIVENESS

Father God of all mercies, I stand before Your presence once again seeking help concerning my unforgiving heart. Lord, You said in Your word, "And when we stand praying, forgive, if we have ought against anyone, that our Father which is in Heaven may forgive us our trespasses. But if we do not forgive, neither will our Heavenly Father forgive us our trespasses" (Mark 11:25-26). I need to be forgiven, and I hold the keys to being forgiven by You if I forgive others.

So, I am asking You, Lord, to assist me because I find it so hard to let go of the people who have offended me or done bad things to me. There is an evil force encouraging me to seek revenge or do something horrible in response to those who hurt me. Lord, please help me to resume control of my thoughts and heart and bring it in alignment with You so that I can easily forgive others and graciously move on with my life.

I am reminded of Your word, "The heart is deceitful above all things, and desperately wicked" (Jeremiah 17:9). You also said that it isn't what goes into a man's mouth that defiles him. Instead, it is what comes out of his mouth that defiles him, because the things that proceed out of his mouth come from his heart.

MY HEART AND FORGIVENESS

For out of the heart proceed evil thoughts, murders, adulteries, fornications, thefts, false witness, and blasphemies. These are the things that defile a person (Matthew 15:11, 17-20).

Lord, my prayer is focusing on my heart because I recall Your words to Samuel the prophet in 1 Samuel 16:7b, "For the Lord does not see the way men see. For men observe the outward appearance and make their judgments from that point. However, the Lord always observes and makes His judgments from the heart of men."

Lord, I do not desire to continue living with an unforgiving, unclean heart. I am tormented day and night by the relentless spirits of offense, unforgiveness, and vindictiveness. I also realize that no matter how much I pretend not to be this way when I am around my fellow Believers, the reality is You are always observing and judging me based on my heart.

With the above understanding in mind, I am asking You, Lord, to create in me a clean heart, O God, and renew the right spirit within me. Cast me not away from Your presence, and take not Your Holy Spirit from me. Restore unto me the joy of my salvation, and uphold me with Your free spirit (Psalm 51:10-12). In the name of Jesus Christ of Nazareth!

PRAYING GODS WORD

Heavenly Father, I thank You for the provisions You have made for me and my children. According to Your word in Psalm 115:14, "I will bless you more and more, you and your children." Heavenly Father, I come in agreement with Your word in Proverbs 11:21b, "the seed of the righteous shall be delivered."

Father I come in agreement with Your word in Psalm 37:25 that promises me that lack will not be my portion. "Once I was young, and now I am old. Yet I have never seen the godly abandoned or their children begging for bread."

Lord I declare while simultaneously agreeing with Your word in Psalm 1:2-3 that says, "If I meditate upon Your word day and night, I 'SHALL' be like a tree planted by the rivers of water that will bring forth fruit in my season, my leaves 'SHALL' not wither and whatsoever I do 'SHALL' prosper."

God Almighty, I bind myself to Your word that cannot lie, and Your word clearly says to me in Proverbs 8:12, "I wisdom dwell with prudence and find out knowledge of witty inventions." Thank You Lord for the knowledge You have set aside just for me to discover witty inventions so that I and my family shall prosper.

PRAYING GODS WORD

Heavenly Father, I bind myself to Your promise that even though weapons may be formed against me, absolutely none of them shall prosper and I exercise my right by condemning every tongue that has risen up against me in judgment according to Isaiah 54:15-17.

Lord, You have said in Your word that the profit of the earth is for all according to Ecclesiastes 5:9. Therefore, I claim my portion in the mighty name of Your Son Jesus Christ! Father, I hold You to Your word that says wisdom and money are a defense. Therefore, I am asking You to bless me with both so that nothing would be able to hinder me in my journey through life as stated in Ecclesiastes 7:12 in the name of Jesus Christ. Amen.

FAITH IN THE WORD OF GOD

Father God, I believe Your word, and I am a believer that Your word is faith because Your word says that faith comes by hearing but not just hearing anything but specifically hearing the word of God according to Romans 10:17. Therefore, I declare Your word back to You which is faith concerning my request to You. You said in Your word that "You will give me houses I did not build and what I did not labor for," according to Deuteronomy 6:11 and Joshua 24:13.

Therefore, I am not asking You for a down payment for my car or home, instead, by faith which is Your word, I am requesting a debt-free home along with a debt-free car because Your word has made it clear to me that You desire to exceed my expectations of You according to Ephesians 3:20.

Father God Almighty, the Creator of heaven and earth, Your word declares that it is IMPOSSIBLE to please or satisfy You without faith as stated in Hebrews 11:6. Therefore, I am bringing my faith to You which is Your word. Your word, which is my faith, says, "the seed of the righteous shall be delivered and that the seed of the righteous shall be mighty upon the earth," as mentioned in Psalm 112:2 and Proverbs 11:21.

FAITH IN THE WORD OF GOD

Again, because I am fully aware that it is always Your desire to exceed whatever it is that I request of You according to Your will, then I pray Your word as it relates to my life and children as Your word says in Psalm 115:14, which again is my faith, "You will increase me more and more, me and my children." Therefore, I pray that I will experience overall blessings in my life in the name of Jesus.

I also pray for my children that not only will they receive good grades and favour in certain areas of their lives, I pray that they would experience overall blessed lives and that You would deliver them in every area of their lives in the name of Your Son Jesus Christ. Amen.

AFFIRMATION PROMISES FOR THE RIGHTEOUS

Heavenly Father, today I declare and decree the promises and benefits that I am entitled to as a righteous person. Therefore, I proclaim the following:

"For the Lord will bless the righteous and with favour will you compass him as with a shield" (Psalms 5:12).

"For the Lord knows the way of the righteous" (Psalms 1:6).

"For God is in the generation of the righteous" (Psalms 14:5).

"Let the lying lips be put to silence, which speak grievous things proudly and contemptuously against the righteous" (Psalms 31:18).

"Be glad in the Lord, and rejoice, you righteous, and shout for joy, all you that are upright in heart" (Psalms 32:11).

"The eyes of the Lord are upon the righteous, and His ears are open to their cry" (Psalms 34:15).

"The righteous cry and the Lord hears, and delivers them out of all their troubles" (Psalms 34:17).

AFFIRMATION PROMISES OF THE RIGHTEOUS

"Many are the afflictions of the righteous, but the Lord delivers him out of them all" (Psalms 34:19).

"Evil shall slay the wicked, and they that hate the righteous shall be desolate" (Psalms 34:21).

"He (God) secures sound wisdom for the righteous. He is a buckler to them that walk uprightly" (Proverbs 2:7).

"For the forward is an abomination to the Lord, but his secret is with the righteous" (Proverbs 3:32).

"The Lord will not suffer the soul of the righteous to famish (starve)" (Proverbs 10:3).

"The mouth of a righteous man is a well of life" (Proverbs 10:11).

"The lips of the righteous feed many" (Proverbs 10:21).

"As the whirlwind passes, so is the wicked no more: but the righteous is an everlasting foundation" (Proverbs 10:25).

"The righteous shall never be moved" (Proverbs 10:30).

AFFIRMATION PROMISES OF THE RIGHTEOUS

""The lips of the righteous know what is acceptable, but the mouth of the wicked speaks forwardness" (Proverbs 10:32).

"The righteous is delivered out of trouble, and the wicked comes in his stead" (Proverbs 11:8).

"Though hand join in hand, the wicked shall not go unpunished, but the seed of the righteous shall be delivered" (Proverbs 11:21).

"The desire of the righteous is only good" (Proverbs 11:23).

"He that trusts in his riches shall fall, but the righteous shall flourish as a branch" (Proverbs 11:28).

"The fruit of the righteous is a tree of life, and he that wins souls is wise" (Proverbs 11:30).

"Behold, the righteous shall be recompensed in the earth, much more the wicked and the sinner" (Proverbs 11:31).

"A man shall not be established by wickedness, but the root of the righteous shall not be moved" (Proverbs 12:3).

"The wicked flees when no one pursues him, but the righteous are bold as a lion" (Proverbs 28:1).

AFFIRMATION PROMISES OF THE RIGHTEOUS

"Whoso causes the righteous to go astray in an evil way. He shall fall himself into his own pit, but the upright shall have good things in possession" (Proverbs 28:10).

"The righteous considers the cause of the poor, but the wicked regard it not" (Proverbs 29:7).

"When the wicked are multiplied, transgressions increase, but the righteous shall see their fall" (Proverbs 29:16).

"Plot not, O wicked man, against the dwelling of the righteous; spoil not his resting place. For a just man falls seven times and gets back up again, but the wicked shall fall into mischief" (Proverbs 24:15-16).

"The righteous man wisely considers his house, but God overthrows the wicked for their wickedness" (Proverbs 21:12).

"The name of the Lord is a strong tower; the righteous runs into it and is safe" (Proverbs 18:10).

"Fools make a mock of sin, but among the righteous is favour" (Proverbs 14:9).

DAILY PRAYERS

BEGINNING OF
EVERYDAY PRAYER

Heavenly Father, amplify Your spirit of discernment in me today that will enable me to see beyond the limitations of my five senses. Reveal to me Lord the traps, lies, deceit, conspiracies and whatever else that has been concocted by Satan and his human agents against me. Father, I pray that the Spirit of Truth, which is Your Holy Spirit, will lead me into all truth in this day and in days to come.

Let Your Holy Spirit convict me of any evil that resides dormant in my heart. Lord, I truly repent of any of Your laws, rules or principles that I have breached. I confess my iniquities, sins, along with my transgressions so that there would be no partition between You and me.

Lord Your word is clear when You said in Proverbs 28:13 that he that hides his sin SHALL NOT PROSPER! "He that covereth his sins shall not prosper: but whoso confesseth and forsaketh them shall have mercy." It is my desire to prosper and not just me alone but also that there would be consistent prosperity among my family members.

BEGINNING OF EVERYDAY PRAYER

Heavenly Father, I now outfit myself and family with the whole armor of God so that we would be able to stand against the wiles of the enemy according to Ephesians 6:11-13.

I also pray that Your angels will encamp around my family and me to also deliver us as You have promised according to Your word in Psalm 34:7 which says, "the angel of the Lord encampeth round about them that fear him, and delivereth them."

I now command to be arrested any and all bad news that was pending to visit me in the physical realm. I further command to be destroyed by Holy Ghost fire every evil covenant that may have been established in my dreams and all evil verbal communication from my mouth. Instead, I decree that life, health, and strength shall be my portion and that of my family on this day.

I decree that no good thing shall be withheld from me according to Your word in Psalm 84:11. "For the Lord God is a sun and shield: the Lord will give grace and glory: no good thing will he withhold from them that walk uprightly."

I decree and stand in complete agreement with Your word according to Psalm 138:8 that says You will perfect all that concerns me. Sickness will not be my portion or that of my family in Jesus' name. I command and declare that every missed opportunity along with every opportunity that was somehow manipulated out of my reach must revisit me in the mighty name of Jesus.

I speak with authority to the spirits of jealousy, hate, deceit, anger, unforgiveness, manipulation and pride that are controlling and influencing my enemies to work against me and my family. I command these spirits to become confused and disgraced by the power of the living God in the mighty name of Jesus Christ. Amen.

I COMMAND THIS DAY

I pray this morning that God will uproot every evil seed planted in my dreams last night and as early as this morning. Every evil dream that has programmed my day for failure and delay in my affairs, I command them to be destroyed and never manifest in the mighty name of Jesus. Every spiritual attack against my job, marriage, family, business, finances, emotions and all that concerns me, I command those plans against me to become frustrated and fail now in the mighty name of Jesus Christ!

I command the exposure of all pending covert attacks against me and my family. I pray that God will clearly reveal all the Judas Iscariots in my life and that he would unseat them by His spiritual fire in the mighty name of Jesus. Every Obeah, witchcraft and voodoo spirits that have been sent or are currently operating in my life that have caused unexplained sickness in my body by disabling my health and frustrating my doctors simply because of their evil spiritual nature; I call for that same angel of the Lord in Second Kings 19:35 that God sent to destroy 185,000 Assyrian enemies of the children of Israel to consume and cause to exist no more the invisible forces operating against me.

I COMMAND THIS DAY

I speak directly to my finances and command the spirit of increase to be released from the spiritual cage it has been placed in by the enemy and I now command the spirit of poverty to take up residence in that cage forever in the name of Jesus Christ. I command the angelic host of peace to arrest and detain all spirits attacking my mind and soul. I command that same angelic host of peace to specifically sentence to spiritual death the spirits of fear, doubt, worry, lack of self-control, insomnia, and fear of the unknown in Jesus' name.

I pray that God would undo the iniquities of my ancestors so that I and generations to come would not be burdened with generational curses. Finally, I decree and declare that God will not only advance me to where I should have been at this point in my life, but all visible and invisible barriers as of this moment are removed by the spiritual advancers of God in the mighty and matchless name of Jesus Christ. AMEN!

EVERYDAY PRAYER WHEN FASTING

Heavenly Father, in the name of Your Son Jesus Christ, I confess all sins that I have committed against You in word, deed, thought and in action. Lord, I repent of all evil that I have done and if there is any evil within me that I'm not aware of, I ask Your forgiveness of those sins and pray that You cleanse me of all evil in the name of Jesus.

Lord, Your word says in 1 Corinthians 6:19-20, that "my body is the temple of the Lord and I must also present my body as a living sacrifice, holy and acceptable unto You." Lord, during this fast in which I am surrendering my body as a living sacrifice unto You, I am asking that You spiritually and physically remove all evil contamination that has been subtly deposited into my body that has caused unexplained sicknesses in my spirit and body in the name of Jesus.

Father, I firmly stand on Your word that will bring about my healing. Lord, Your word says in Isaiah 41:10, "Fear thou not; for I [am] with thee: be not dismayed; for I [am] thy God. I will strengthen thee; yea, I will help thee; yea, I will uphold thee with the right hand of my righteousness."

EVERYDAY PRAYER WHEN FASTING

Lord, I bind myself to Your word written in Jeremiah 17:14 that says, "Heal me, O LORD, and I shall be healed; save me, and I shall be saved: for thou [art] my praise."

Father God, Your word says in Proverbs 18:21 that death and life are in the power of my tongue. Therefore, I speak death to all spiritual and physical contamination operating in my body. I command all residue of any contamination to be passed out of me in the mighty name of Your Son Jesus Christ. Lord, You said that we should remind You of Your word. Therefore, I am reminding You of Your word that says in Jeremiah 33:6, "Behold, I will bring it health and cure, and I will cure them and will reveal unto them the abundance of peace and truth."

Father, Your word says in Philippians 4:19, "You will supply all my needs according to Your riches in glory by Christ Jesus." So, I am asking You to provide me with complete healing and deliverance to my spirit, soul, and body in the name of Your Son Jesus Christ. Lord, I am reminding You again of Your word as written in Isaiah 54:17 telling me that no weapon formed against me shall prosper and I have condemned all tongues that have risen up against me in judgment.

EVERYDAY PRAYER WHEN FASTING

Therefore, I am in a state of expectancy from You in the mighty name of Your Son Jesus Christ. Lord, You said in Isaiah 57:18 that You have seen my ways and You will heal me. You promised that You would lead me and restore comfort unto me, Your mourner.

Finally, Heavenly Father, I am digging my faith deeper into the foundation of Your word. The word says in Isaiah 53:5, "But he was wounded for our transgressions, he was bruised for our iniquities. The chastisement of our peace was upon him, and with his stripes, we are healed."

Therefore, I decree and declare the complete restoration of my spirit, mind, body, and whatever else is in my system. I send the fire of God against all contamination and command it to be eliminated from my body in the name of Jesus Christ, which is the name above all names. Amen!

DREAM
PRAYERS

PRAYER AGAINST FORGETTING DREAMS

Heavenly Father and Lord of all creation, I come before You seeking spiritual assistance in combating the spirits of forgetfulness, confusion, frustration, and fatigue that have been launched against the knowledge and revelation You have given to me in my dreams. Father, Your spiritual law declares that it is the result of a lack of knowledge that the people of God are destroyed according to Hosea 4:6.

Therefore, Heavenly Father, destroy the invisible forces that are attempting to hijack this vital knowledge, You have released to me in my dreams. Lord, I stand and bind myself to Your word that clearly says, "the memory of the just is blessed" according to Proverbs 10:7. I declare that my memory is indeed blessed and that I am able to recall all that You have released to me spiritually.

Father, I now pray Your word over my mind and memory. I am asking that You release to me according to Your word, the spirit of wisdom, knowledge, and understanding as written in Isaiah 11:2 so that I will be able to understand exactly what You are saying to me or pointing out to me via my dreams.

PRAYER AGAINST FORGETTING DREAMS

Finally, Heavenly Father, I pray and come in agreement with Your servant the Apostle Paul, who prayed that the eyes of my understanding be enlightened, so that I would know the hope of what You have called me to according to Ephesians 1:18. I stand on Your word as it relates to my memory, and Your word says in Proverbs 10:7, "The memory of the just is blessed." I pray this in the mighty name of Jesus! Amen.

Note: After ending such a prayer just sit or find a relaxed quiet position and allow the angels of the Lord, who respond to the word of God according to Psalm 103:20 to begin to fight on your behalf. I promise you, that in the coming weeks you will start to recall your dreams without effort.

PRAYER FOR CANCELLING AGREEMENT WITH A DREAM

Father God, I come to You in the name of Your Son Jesus Christ. Father, I know I just had a dream, but I don't remember anything of it, nor do I understand the dream that I just woke up from. Therefore, I cancel everything of that dream that is not of You. I cancel whatever evil seed or evil covenant that Satan had established or planted in my dream, every visible and invisible plan, plot, device and scheme. I at this moment solemnly reject, renounce, rebuke and ultimately cancel it by the blood of Jesus Christ.

I also cancel any short or long-term effect of evil that Satan and his agents had previously planted in my life, including any evil covenants that would have been subtly forged in that dream. I disassociate myself from it now. I cancel, I reject, I renounce, I cancel all agreements that are not with You Father. Father, I disassociate myself from all the powers of the kingdom of darkness that are related to that dream.

It shall not take shape in my life, the life of my family members or anyone that dream is pertaining to this, I declare in the mighty and matchless name of Your Son and my savior Jesus Christ. Amen.

PRAYER FOR COMING IN AGREEMENT WITH A DREAM

Father God, if this dream is from You, I bind myself to what You desire for my life because according to Your word in Jeremiah 29:11 it says, "Your thoughts towards me are good and not evil and that I will have an expected end." Therefore, I can trust You that if the dream is from You then it is something to benefit me.

Reveal to me what that is and I come wholeheartedly in agreement with it in Jesus' name. Now Lord, as You've instructed, I pray the whole armor of God over my entire being, so that I will now be able to stand against the wiles of the devil and to also stand in the evil day, according to Ephesians 6:11-13. I now enact Psalm 91:11-12 where You've promised that, "You've given Your angels charge over me to keep me in all my ways and that if I as much as dash my foot against a stone they will gather me in their arms."

I further speak to the spirit realm that must submit to Your word, that absolutely no weapon that has or will ever be formed against me shall prosper. I wholeheartedly condemn every evil tongue, every evil voice, every evil sacrifice along with every evil altar speaking against my destiny and they are to be consumed by Holy Ghost fire in the mighty name of Jesus Christ, according to Isaiah 54:17. Amen.

20 BIBLE VERSES TO CANCEL BAD DREAMS

1). Matthew 18:18, "Verily I say unto you, Whatsoever ye shall bind on earth shall be bound in heaven: and whatsoever ye shall loose on earth shall be loosed in heaven."

2). Luke 10:19, "Behold, I give unto you power to tread on serpents and scorpions, and over all the power of the enemy: and nothing shall by any means hurt you."

3). Psalm 27:1-2, "The Lord is my light and my salvation; whom shall I fear? The Lord is the strength of my life; of whom shall I be afraid? When the wicked, even mine enemies and my foes, came upon me to eat up my flesh, they stumbled and fell."

4). Revelation 12:11, "And they overcame him by the blood of the Lamb, and by the word of their testimony; and they loved not their lives unto the death."

5). Mark 11:23, "For verily I say unto you, That whosoever shall say unto this mountain, Be thou removed, and be thou cast into the sea; and shall not doubt in his heart, but shall believe that those things which he saith shall come to pass; he shall have whatsoever he saith."

6). John 10:10, "The thief cometh not, but for to steal, and to kill, and to destroy: I am come that they might have life, and that they might have [it] more abundantly."

7). Proverbs 3:24, "When thou liest down, thou shalt not be afraid: yea, thou shalt lie down, and thy sleep shall be sweet."

8). Isaiah 28:18, "And your covenant with death shall be disannulled, and your agreement with hell shall not stand; when the overflowing scourge shall pass through, then ye shall be trodden down by it."

9). Isaiah 59:19, "So shall they fear the name of the Lord from the west, and His glory from the rising of the sun. When the enemy shall come in like a flood, the Spirit of the Lord shall lift up a standard against him."

10). 2 Timothy 1:7, "For God hath not given us the spirit of fear; but of power, and of love, and of a sound mind."

11). James 4:7, "Submit yourselves therefore to God. Resist the devil, and he will flee from you."

12). Lamentations 3:37, "Who is he that saith, and it cometh to pass, when the Lord commandeth it not?"

13). Joel 2:21, "Fear not, O land; be glad and rejoice: for the Lord will do great things."

14). Ephesians 6:12, "For we wrestle not against flesh and blood, but against principalities, against powers, against the rulers of the darkness of this world, against spiritual wickedness in high places."

15). Mark 3:27, "No man can enter into a strong man's house, and spoil his goods, except he will first bind the strong man; and then he will spoil his house."

16). Galatians 3:13, "Christ hath redeemed us from the curse of the law, being made a curse for us: for it is written, Cursed is every one that hangeth on a tree:"

17). Psalm 118:12, "They compassed me about like bees; they are quenched as the fire of thorns: for in the name of the LORD I will destroy them."

18). Isaiah 54:17, "No weapon that is formed against thee shall prosper; and every tongue that shall rise against thee in judgment thou shalt condemn. This is the heritage of the servants of the LORD, and their righteousness is of me, saith the LORD."

19). Numbers 23:23, "Surely there is no enchantment against Jacob, neither is there any divination against Israel: according to this time it shall be said of Jacob and of Israel, What hath God wrought!"

20). Deuteronomy 28:7, "The LORD shall cause thine enemies that rise up against thee to be smitten before thy face: they shall come out against thee one way, and flee before thee seven ways." Amen.

PRAYERS
FOR
THE MIND

DELIVERANCE OF THE MIND

Heavenly Father, in the name of Your Son Jesus Christ, I, Pastor Kevin L.A. Ewing, am certain that it is You that has prompted in my spirit to record this prayer for the readers. I pray for those that are reading this prayer and the ones that need their minds delivered as it relates to mental illness and mental challenges. Firstly, I cover all those reading this prayer with the whole armor of God. Secondly, I dispatch the warring angels of the Lord to wage war on the demonic host and legions that have been assigned against their minds. Thirdly, I cover their thoughts, ideas, thinking processes and imagination with the precious blood of Jesus Christ in the name of Jesus.

Pray this prayer over Your mind and Yourself:

Heavenly Father, I call upon You, whom Your word has described as a consuming fire, to burn at the very root every spirit of depression, mental dullness, forgetfulness, mind blankness, confusion, incoherence, fear, suicide, abnormal thinking of death, worry, spirits of heaviness, sexually perverted thoughts, violence, unforgiveness, and bitterness. Father, I bind the spirits of laziness, procrastination, the lack of will power, the lack of might, the lack of courage and the lack of determination in the name of Jesus!

DELIVERANCE OF THE MIND

Father in the name of Your Son Jesus Christ, I pray that You rain down fire like in the days of Sodom and Gomorrah upon every spirit that has been consistently attacking my mind, in particular in the areas of doubting Your word, the reading of Your word, and most of all not being able to focus on Your word. I command the spirits of anxiety and panic attacks to die in the name of Jesus Christ.

Lord where I have received any type of devastating news, whether it be through the loss of a loved one, a broken marriage, divorce, an unwelcome doctor's report, or where the power of darkness has come in the form of the spirit of grief to torment me, I command all these spirits and the power of darkness that have been tormenting me in my mind and body to die and be cast into the abyss in the name of Jesus Christ!

Father, I attack the spirit of uncertainty with spiritual brute force which is Your word that says in Romans 8:31, IF YOU (GOD) BE FOR US, WHO CAN BE AGAINST US! I now call upon the angels of the Lord who have been given charge over me to keep me in all my ways to go forth and to take back what the enemy has stolen from me mentally and spiritually in the name of Jesus.

DELIVERANCE OF THE MIND

I command Satan, whom God has said his sole purpose towards me is to kill, steal and to destroy. I command Satan to return to me everything that he has stolen in the name of Jesus Christ.

Heavenly Father, Your word in Proverbs 6:31, gives me the legal right to command what has been taken from me when it said that if the thief (Satan) be found he must restore sevenfold of what he has stolen. God, I thank You that though I may be flowing in tears concerning my mental state, You have heard my inward and outward cries. You indeed are an on-time God and the One who answers the prayers of His people.

Finally Heavenly Father, I want to thank You in advance, for the mind that is in Christ Jesus is operating in me in the name of Jesus. Thank You in advance for the soundness of my mind, the ability to focus, concentrate, make a sound decision and to possess a sense of freedom in my thoughts in the name of Jesus.

Thank You for pure, pleasant imagination and the ability to freely think positively. Thank You for giving me the power to relinquish my mind of perverted, sexual, immoral thoughts, negativity, evil imaginations, and thinking evil of others. I ask these things and believe they are done by faith in the name of Your Son Jesus Christ Amen!

DELIVERANCE OF THE MIND

Readers of this prayer: If you are tired of being tormented by the enemy I suggest you copy this prayer and repeat it at least three times a day. Remember we are in a battle with who has the advantage of seeing us, but it is not common for us to see them. However, prayer acts as a sword in the spirit, especially prayers saturated with the word of God. I come in agreement with all of you that pray this prayer in the name of Jesus. Amen. Pastor Kevin L.A. Ewing.

PRAYER AGAINST THE SPIRIT OF DEPRESSION

Heavenly Father, I thank You for revealing to me that depression is a spirit and not just an emotion. Therefore, I will discontinue treating this spirit as a feeling and I will start attacking it from the root, which is spiritual. I am now asking You to destroy by fire the root of depression, which I now know to be the spirit of depression. Spirit of depression, I refuse to ignorantly work along with You in keeping myself depressed via negative thoughts, grieving over things that I cannot change, the loss of a job, the loss of a business, the loss of an investment, the loss of a loved one, a broken marriage, disappointing kids, failures, any form of discouraging and disappointing experiences in the name of Jesus!

Instead, I come in total agreement with the word of God that says in 1 Thessalonians 5:18, I must give thanks in all things because this is the will of God in Christ Jesus concerning me at this point in my life. Lord, even though I cannot understand the reason behind this negative and perplexing matter that the spirit of depression has taken full advantage of, I will continue to hold on and speak Your word that clearly says in Romans 8:28, "And we know that all things work together for good to them that love God, to them who are the called according to His purpose."

PRAYER AGAINST THE SPIRIT OF DEPRESSION

Finally, Heavenly Father, I speak to the spirit of depression via the authority that You have given me; therefore, I say to the spirit of depression, "God Almighty has given me the garment of praise for the spirit of heaviness," according to Isaiah 61:3. Spirit of depression, you have been identified and exposed! I curse you and all your devices! I reject you in every area of my life in the mighty name of Jesus.

I dispatch the angelic host to destroy all your efforts against me in the name of Jesus! Spirit of depression, the Lord said that He, (Christ Jesus) has become a curse for me according to Galatians 3:13. Therefore, I command every generational curse of depression operating in my life and in the lives of my family to be broken at this very moment in the mighty and matchless name of Jesus Christ! Amen.

PRAYER AGAINST THE SPIRIT OF CONFUSION

I come to You Lord, reminding You of Your word according to 1 Corinthians 14:33 that says, "You are not the author of confusion." Therefore, I command the spirit of confusion that has been challenging me to be destroyed by Your spiritual fire in the name of Jesus Christ! Heavenly Father, Your word declares in James 3:16 that confusion is the product or result of envy and strife.

Lord, I stand on Your word from Hebrews 4:12, which You said is "likened to a sword," and I sever the root of this spirit of confusion, which is from envy and strife. I command envy, strife, and the spirit of confusion to be disabled permanently in my life in the mighty name of Jesus Christ!

Lord, cover me with the blood of Jesus Christ and with the whole armor of God. Cover me to the point that envy, strife, and confusion will not know where to go, who to talk to, or what to do next in the name of Jesus.

Spirit of confusion, I curse you in the name of Jesus Christ and command you to leave my life permanently in the mighty name of Jesus Christ!

PRAYER AGAINST THE SPIRIT OF CONFUSION

Now Lord, I pray that You would replace that void that the spirit of confusion has left with Your spirit of wisdom, knowledge, understanding, direction, hope, motivation, inspiration and most of all Your Spirit of TRUTH in the matchless name of Jesus Christ! Amen.

PRAYERS FOR PEACE

Father God, if there is ever a time when I need you, it is now. I feel so emotional, confused, and unable to gain control of the relentless thoughts that are trafficking in and out of my mind. Therefore, Lord, I confess and repent of my sins, both known and unknown. I am truly sorry for what I have done, and I believe by faith that I am forgiven and that you have cleansed me of all unrighteousness (1 John 1:9).

Lord, I am aware that my struggle is primarily spiritual, so I have decided to outfit myself with the whole armor of God, emphasizing the sword of the spirit, which is your word. As a result, I decree and declare that the God of Abraham, Isaac, and Jacob did not give me a spirit of fear but of love, power, and a sound mind. I reject every opposing spirit in my mind and command it to leave now in the name of Jesus Christ! I cling to the word of God that says, "Peace, peace to him who is far off, and to him who is near," says the Lord, "and I will heal him" (Isaiah 57:19).

Father, according to your word in Psalm 103:20, your angels listen to the voice of your word and do your commandments. By the authority of your word, Father, I now deploy the angelic host you have assigned to me through the word of God, according to Psalm 34:7 and Psalm 91:11-12.

PRAYERS FOR PEACE

As I declare the scriptures of peace, I am convinced that the angels of the Lord must minister to me as an heir of salvation, according to Hebrews 1:13-14. I declare, "Great peace have they that love thy law, and nothing should offend them" (Psalms 119:165).

I declare and decree, "God will keep me in perfect peace as long as I continue to retain Him in my thoughts" (Isaiah 26:3). I receive the peace of God, which surpasses all understanding. This same peace will keep my heart and mind through Christ Jesus" (Philippians 4:7). I will hear what God the Lord has spoken, for He will speak peace unto His people and to His saints" (Psalms 85:8). I will let the peace of God rule in my heart because I am a part of the body of Christ, and I am thankful" (Colossians 3:15).

I receive the word of God, "Now the Lord of peace himself gives me peace always by all means" (2 Thessalonians 3:16). Observe the perfect man and behold the upright, for the end of that man is peace" (Psalm 37:37). I decree and declare that my faith has saved me, and I will now go forward in peace" (Luke 7:50). I decree and declare that the works of my righteousness shall produce peace, and the effects of righteousness will equate to quietness and assurance forever" (Isaiah 32:17).

PRAYERS FOR PEACE

I receive and declare the words of the Lord, "Peace I leave with you; my peace I give to you. Not as the world gives do I give to you. Let not your hearts be troubled, neither let them be afraid" (John 14:27). I receive the word of the Lord, "The Lord bless thee and keep thee. The Lord make His face shine upon thee and be gracious unto thee. The Lord lifts His countenance upon thee and gives thee peace" (Numbers 6:24-26). I decree and declare, "The fruit of righteousness is sown in peace of them that make peace" (James 3:18).

Heavenly Father, I have declared Your word, and I believe with all my heart, mind, spirit, and soul that the angels You have given charge over me have been deployed to ensure that Your word comes to pass. I seal this prayer with Your word that says, "And this is the confidence that we have in Him, that if we ask anything according to His will, He hears us. If we know that He hears us, whatsoever we ask, we know that we have the petitions that we desire of Him" (1 John 5:14-15). In the name of Jesus Christ of Nazareth!

PRAYER AGAINST LIMITATION

Heavenly Father, please forgive every sin in my life that I have committed knowingly and unknowingly that is limiting me. Oh Lord have mercy on me and wash me clean in the blood of Jesus. I now remove every limitation I have placed on God for the direction of my life in Jesus' name. I break every visible and invisible yoke of limitation upon my life in Jesus' name. Father, deliver me from all limiting forces operating in my life today in Jesus' name.

I uproot every thought of littleness in my mind in Jesus' name. Anything in my family house that has covenanted me to non-achievement, be broken in Jesus' name. Any spoken statement or written code roaming about creation affecting my rising up, be withdrawn in Jesus' name. Any sacrifice or token offered periodically to renew limitations in my life and work, burn by fire in Jesus' name.

Anything in my foundation that has subjected my life to struggles and contention, be destroyed in Jesus' name. Arrows of endless and fruitless struggles fired into my life, come out in Jesus' name. Every satanic limitation in my life, be demolished in Jesus' name. O Lord, by the blood of Jesus uproot every seed of limitation in my life by fire in Jesus' name.

PRAYER AGAINST LIMITATION

Resurrection Power of God, visit me now and destroy every seal of limitation in my life. Our ancestors have also obeyed, honored Your laws and covenants and they are now dead. However, we that are alive will receive of the blessings they have left in place in the mighty and matchless name of Your Son and my Savior Jesus Christ. Amen!

Lord, let every evil hand limiting my progress be roasted by fire in Jesus' name. Let every stone or obstacle of limitation placed by my enemies be rolled away permanently now in the mighty name of Jesus. Every spirit of impossibility from my ancestral background, die in Jesus' name. Every household covenant operating in my life to limit my destiny, scatter in Jesus' name. Heavenly Father, destroy every weapon of limitation working against my destiny in Jesus' name. I command every demonic sanction and embargo over my destiny to be lifted at once in Jesus' name.

Let every wicked law operating against me be overthrown now in Jesus' name. I resist every attempt to preserve me in poverty and littleness in Jesus' name. Every obstacle hindering my progress, my prayer life, and my divine assignment be destroyed by fire in Jesus' name.

PRAYER AGAINST LIMITATION

Father, give me a hunger for the truth of Your word. Fill me with truth and understanding. I come out of any cage of the enemy limiting my progress right now in Jesus' name. I speak to my destiny to rise up from every valley of limitation today and begin to move forward in the name of Jesus. I declare that I am a no-limit person in Jesus' name. My Heavenly Father divinely separates me from every friendly and unfriendly friend serving as a channel of limitation in my life and I receive maximum support for maximum performance in Jesus' name.

Heavenly Father, go ahead and fulfill Your plans for my life to the fullest in Jesus' name. I declare that from today no good thing shall be impossible in my life in the name of Jesus. By the power of God, I receive the supernatural empowerment to be unlimited from today in Jesus' name. I decree and declare that I am delivered from the spirits of limitation, frustration, and stagnation. Henceforth, my life will radiate the glory of God in the name of Jesus! Thank You Lord for answered prayers. Amen.

PRAYERS FOR BLESSINGS

I NEED FAVOUR NOW

Heavenly Father, I repent of all the sins, iniquities, and transgressions, known and unknown, that I have committed against You. I have initiated the process of You forgiving me by forgiving others, according to Mark 11:25. Lord, there are some matters before me for which human assistance has become exhausted. Therefore, I seek Your favour, which transcends human understanding. Your word says, "Your anger endures for a moment, but in Your favour is life," Psalm 30:5.

Heavenly Father, I receive Your command that spoke directly to me when You said, "That I must not forsake mercy neither truth. Instead, I must bind them (mercy and truth) around my neck and write it upon the table of my heart. By doing this, I shall find favour and good understanding before God and man," Proverbs 3:3-4. Lord, I am so grateful for this spiritual protocol to produce favour in my life.

Father, I am so fascinated by Your spiritual rules that will produce favour in my life. Therefore, I lay claim to Your word that says, "A good man shall obtain favour from the Lord," Proverbs 12:2. "He that diligently seeks good shall procure favour," Proverbs 11:27. "Good understanding gives favour," Proverbs 13:15.

I NEED FAVOUR NOW

Lord, I sink my faith into Your word that says, "Among the righteous, there is favour," Proverbs 14:9. Thank You, Lord, for the favour that comes built into my marriage. "He that finds a wife finds a good thing and obtains favour of the Lord," Proverbs 18:22. Father, I understand that if I desire favour from You, I must ensure that I show favour to others. "A good man shows favour and lends to others; he guides his affairs with discretion," Psalm 112:5. I have intreated thy favour with my whole heart. Please be merciful unto me according to thy word, Psalm 119:58.

Thank You, Lord, that there is a set time that You have appointed supernatural favour for my life. "Thou shall arise and have mercy upon Zion. For the time to favour her, yea, the set time has come," Psalm 102:13. I bless You, Father, once again for my set time of favour.

Father, I am again reminding You of Your word that says, "For thou, Lord, will bless the righteous; with favour, will thou compass him like a shield," Psalm 5:12. Your words are true and so comforting. I bind my spirit, soul, and body to Your precious word. Your word is my life, it is the strength of my life. Therefore, I receive every word that comes from You, my precious Savior, Redeemer, and King.

I NEED FAVOUR NOW

Now, Father, I seal this prayer with my confidence in Your word that said, "Let them shout for joy that favour my righteous cause; yea, let them say continually, let the Lord be magnified, who has pleasure in the prosperity of His servant," in the name of Jesus Christ, Psalm 35:27.

PRAYER FOR FINANCIAL RELEASE AND RELIEF

Dear God of Abraham, Isaac, and Jacob, I come before You once again, following Your instructions by not leaning on my own understanding. In all my ways, I choose to acknowledge You so that You can direct my path, Proverbs 3:5-6. Father, I believe Your word that says, "The profit of the Earth is for all" Ecclesiastes 5:9. However, Lord, the thief whose job is to kill, steal, and destroy has robbed me of my earthly profits.

Firstly, I submit to Your word that commands us to give thanks in all things, for this is the will of God in Christ Jesus concerning us, I Thessalonians 5:18. Lord, while I cannot understand how this could equate to Your will for me, nevertheless, I choose to be more focused on You than any spirits that are stealing from me.

Father, as usual, I will now declare and engage Your spiritual laws to challenge what has been challenging me spiritually not to prosper. Your word says, "Whosoever gives to the poor shall not lack" Proverbs 28:27. Lord, help me to be consistent in meeting the needs of those that cannot help themselves.

PRAYER FOR FINANCIAL RELEASE AND RELIEF

Amplify my spirit of discernment so that I would be confident in whom You are directing me to bless. "A faithful man shall abound with blessings" Proverbs 28:20. Father, thank You for reminding me that my commitment to Your divine will will generate blessings for me.

So, Father, empower me with the spirit of commitment and faithfulness to Your word. Lord, I thank You that the wealth of the wicked will be transferred to me, the just, Proverbs 13:22, and I know that the evidence of my faithfulness must produce fruit. I stand in confidence of Proverbs 11:25, which says, "The liberal soul shall become wealthy, and he that assists others, one day someone will assist him." Your word says, "Money answers all things" Ecclesiastes 10:19, so I pray that You would command the blessings to my life that will generate the finances needed.

I pray that before You release those finances, Father, You would give me a spirit of stewardship and management to better manage the resources that will be released into my life. Heavenly Father, I truly repent for all the opportunities You made possible in the past to bless me. However, due to my lack of spiritual knowledge, I dismissed them. Such as not meeting the needs of those whom You've sent seeking help from me when I was able to assist.

PRAYER FOR FINANCIAL RELEASE AND RELIEF

Now, it is clear to me that one of the reasons for my current position of lack is, "Whoever dismisses the cry of the poor, he also shall cry himself, but shall not be heard" Proverbs 21:13. Lord, I promise that as You pull me out of this pit of lack, not only will I place emphasis on meeting the needs of the poor, but I will make them a priority in my giving according to Your word.

Jesus said, "When you give lunch or food, do not invite your friends, your brothers and sisters, relatives or your rich neighbors. Instead, invite or give initially to the poor, cripple, the lame, and blind and you will be blessed. Although they cannot repay you" Luke 14:12-14. Again, Heavenly Father, please forgive me. I was not aware of such spiritual laws that have clearly determined my financial destiny.

Going forward, Father, now that my mind is renewed concerning Your spiritual rules of prosperity, according to Romans 12:2, I will comply with Your Spirit to assist others. "For it is God who works in us both to will and to do for His good pleasure" Philippians 2:13. Thank You, thank You, thank You, my sweet Jesus Christ of Nazareth, for giving me another chance at this and being so patient. You are a patient, merciful, and loving God. I bless and honor the day I said yes to You.

PRAYER FOR FINANCIAL RELEASE AND RELIEF

I bless You for the many benefits that come along with serving. I seal this prayer with the word of God that says, "Whatever things you ask when you pray, believe that you receive them, and you will have them" in the name of Jesus Christ, Mark 11:24.

DOORS OF BLESSINGS

Heavenly Father, I stand humbly in Your presence, as usual, asking for Your mercy and forgiveness for my sins, iniquities, and transgressions. Secondly, I thank You for the gift of life as well as Your gift of salvation. Lord, today I have made the decision to access the spiritual blessings You have stored for me in heavenly places (Ephesians 1:3). You said, "And it shall come to pass, if I would listen diligently unto the voice of the Lord thy God, to observe and do all His commandments which He has commanded me this day, the Lord thy God will set me on high above all nations of the earth, and these blessings shall come on me and overtake me if I would listen unto the voice of the Lord my God" (Deuteronomy 28:1-2).

Father, I bind myself to Your word and commit to Your commandments, rules, laws, and principles. Now, by faith, I declare and decree that I am blessed in my body, spirit, and soul. I am blessed on my job, my marriage is blessed, and I am blessed in my ministry. I am blessed in abundance financially. Through obedience to Your word, it has produced the fruit of blessing that has made me the head and not the tail. I am and will continue to be above only and not beneath in the name of Jesus Christ.

DOORS OF BLESSINGS

Lord, You said in Your word that You will command the blessings upon me in my storehouses (bank accounts) and in everything that I set my hand to. You further promised that You will bless the properties that You have given me (Deuteronomy 28:8) Father, You said that blessings are automatically levied on me if I walk not in the counsel of the ungodly, nor stand in the way of sinners, nor keep company with the proud (Psalm 1:1).

Father, I have received a commandment from You to bless those that curse me (Luke 6:28), which I will continue to do. In turn, You promised me that You will bless those that bless me and curse those that curse me (Genesis 12:3). I receive Your word that says, "Blessed is he that considers the poor: the Lord will deliver him in time of trouble.

The Lord will preserve him and keep him alive, and he shall be blessed upon the earth. The Lord will not deliver him unto the will of his enemies. The Lord will strengthen this blessed man on his sick bed and restore him from his bed of illness" (Psalm 41:1-3).

DOORS OF BLESSINGS

My God, my King, my shield, and buckler, I firmly stand on Your word that says, "Blessed is the man that fears the Lord and delights greatly in His commandments." Father, I thank You because You said, "Blessed is the man whose strength is in Thee" (Psalm 84:5).

Lord, I relish in Your divine promise that says, "Blessed is the man that trusts in the Lord, and whose hope the Lord is. For he shall be like a tree planted by the waters that spreads out her roots by the river. This blessed man shall not fear when the trouble of life comes. Instead, his leaves shall be green, and he shall not be afraid in the year of recession, neither shall this blessed man cease from yielding fruit" (Jeremiah 17:7-8).

Finally, Father, please help me stay focused on Your will, because I realize that by doing Your will, You reward us with blessings. So, I thank You, honor You, and praise You for Your endless blessings in the name of Your Son and my Savior, Jesus Christ. Amen!

COMMANDING THE EARTH AND ITS INHABITANTS TO WORK IN YOUR FAVOUR

Every evil voice speaking against the favour and mercy that God has impressed upon others to grant me, let that favour and mercy spring forth without delay in the mighty name of Jesus Christ! Every institution or person that has promised to assist me, may the spirit of commitment overwhelm them to follow through on their promises in Jesus' name!

Every opportunity that has somehow missed me, or was secretly stolen or manipulated away from me, may those opportunities revisit me in greater portions in the mighty name of Jesus Christ! May the evil powers behind every block in my life be permanently disabled and become a stepping stone in elevating me to my God intended destiny in the matchless name of Jesus Christ!

Finally, spiritual law dictates in Ecclesiastes: 5:9, "The profit of the earth is for all." Therefore, Lord, I command the earth to release and give up my portions of its profits according to Your word in the mighty name of Jesus Christ! As written in Jeremiah 22:29, "O earth, earth, earth, HEAR THE WORD OF THE LORD."

Heavenly Father, I pray that You release my portion in the earth that's being held up by the enemy in the name of Your Son Jesus Christ! As it is written in Isaiah 61:7, "For your shame, ye shall have double, and for confusion, they shall rejoice in their portion: therefore in their land, they shall possess the double: everlasting joy shall be unto them."

MY PORTION ON EARTH

Success is my portion.

Wealth is my portion.

Health is my portion.

Wisdom is my portion.

Understanding is my portion.

Righteousness is my portion.

Knowledge is my portion.

Insight is my portion.

Happiness is my portion.

Favour is my portion.

The soundness of mind is my portion.

Understanding mysteries is my portion.

My children's success is my portion.

COMMANDING THE EARTH AND ITS INHABITANTS...

Lord, let the Angelic host that You've given charge over me, arrest and take back my portion from the demonic army of robbers in the name of Jesus Christ! Beginning this day and in days to come, I expect to experience all the tangible portions that belong to me from the earth in the name of Jesus Christ! Amen.

PRAYERS
FOR
FAMILY

PRAYER FOR CHILDREN

Heavenly Father, I approach Your throne of grace and mercy today with praises and thanksgiving for Your many blessings bestowed upon me. As usual, I repent of all my sins, iniquities, and transgressions, and by faith, I know You have forgiven me.

Lord, I present my children before You, reminding You of the many promises You gave me concerning them. Your word says, "God is not a man, that He should lie; neither the son of man, that He should repent: hath He said, and shall He not do it? or hath He spoken, and shall He not make it good? Numbers 23:19.

Father, as Hannah presented her son, Samuel, back to You, 1 Samuel 1:26-28. Today, I do likewise and present my child/children back to You. I declare and decree over my child/children's life. A life of commitment, honor, and love for the God of Abraham, Isaac, and Jacob. I sincerely pray that not only will my child/children fulfill and complete their God-ordained purpose, but they will never abandon the covenant they committed to when they accepted the gift of salvation.

PRAYER FOR CHILDREN

I stand on the word of God that says, "Believe on the Lord Jesus Christ, and thou shalt be saved, and thy house" Acts 16:31. Father, You promised, "All my children shall be taught of the Lord, and great shall be the peace of my children," Isaiah 54:13. Lord, You are so great and so awesome; I receive this promise for my children with great appreciation, "For I will pour water upon him that is thirsty and floods upon the dry grounds. I will pour my Spirit upon thy seed, and my blessings upon thy offspring," Isaiah 44:3.

Heavenly Father, I receive Your word that says, "Thy wife shall be as a faithful vine by the sides of thine house. Thy children like olive plants round about thy table," Psalms 128:3. Lord, You promised, "Children are the heritage of the Lord, and the fruit of the womb is His reward. As arrows are in the hand of a mighty man. So, are children of the youth. Happy is the man that has his quiver full of them: they shall not be ashamed, but they shall speak with the enemies in the gate," Psalms 127:3-5.

Father, I am grateful that one of the benefits of myself being righteous through the acceptance of Your son Jesus Christ. My children are guaranteed deliverance according to Your word.

PRAYER FOR CHILDREN

"Though hand join in hand, the wicked shall not go unpunished, but the seed of the righteous shall be delivered," Proverbs 11:21. Father, I thank You in advance for my children's deliverance.

Lord, I am so thankful for Your promise, which incorporates my child/children, saying, "Praise ye the Lord. Blessed is the man that fears the Lord and delights greatly in His commandments. His seed shall be mighty upon the earth, and the generation of the upright shall be blessed," Psalms 112:1-2.

My decree and declare that my child/children's days will be long upon the earth because they honor their father and mother, Ephesians 6:1-3. Lord, Your word says that a child left to themselves shall bring their parents to shame," Proverbs 29:15. Lord, I commit to You to always be there for my child/children and support them according to Your word.

Your word says, "A fool despises his Father's instructions, but he that regards reproof is prudent," Proverbs 15:5. I decree that my child/children are obedient and, most of all, prudent! I shall rejoice, and I will be inundated with joy because the word of God says, "The Father of the righteous shall rejoice, and he that has a wise child shall have joy of him.

PRAYER FOR CHILDREN

Thy Father and mother shall be glad, and she that bare thee shall rejoice", Proverbs 23:24,25. Lord, help me to be consistent with Your word when guiding and advising my child/children so that they will not depart from their Godly upbringing as they grow, as Your word says in Proverbs 22:6. The more I meditate on Your word, Lord, the more I become aware of how my handling of Your word impacts the life of my children.

You said, "Oh, that their hearts would be inclined to fear me and keep all my commands always so that it might go well with them and their children forever" in Deuteronomy 5:29. Deuteronomy 30:19 said, "I call heaven and earth to record this day against you, that I have set before you life and death, blessing and cursing: therefore choose life, that both thou and thy seed may live."

Father, once again, I am so grateful for the encouraging promises You have given me concerning my child/children. Now that I understand the spiritual laws that dictate death and life are in the power of my words, Proverbs 18:21, I repent, renounce, denounce, and divorce my children from every evil word I have spoken over their lives.

PRAYER FOR CHILDREN

I further break every bloodline, ancestral, and generational curse over their lives, and I pray that You, O Lord, will catapult them into their divine destiny.

I declare that my child/children are the head and not the tail, they are above only and never beneath, and will obey God's word, Deuteronomy 28:13. Through my child/children's obedience to the word of God, "The Lord shall command the blessing upon thee in thy storehouses, and in all that thou settest thine hand unto; and he shall bless thee in the land which the Lord thy God giveth thee," Deuteronomy 28:8.

I decree and declare that my child/children will marry the person whom God had appointed for them before the foundation of the world. My children will never divorce and will only be separated from their union through death. My child/children will have a happy home with blessed children, and they will always work in synergy with their spouses and children in resolving their issues.

I bind every spirit of infirmity assigned by the enemy and decree excellent health over my current and future generations of children.

PRAYER FOR CHILDREN

Poverty and shame will not be participants in their lives. Instead, they will have more than enough and always be a blessing to others. I pray that because of their generosity in giving to the less fortunate, Psalms 41:1-3 will always be their portion: "Blessed is he that considereth the poor: the Lord will deliver him in time of trouble.

The Lord will preserve and keep him alive, and he shall be blessed upon the earth: and thou wilt not deliver him unto the will of his enemies. The Lord will strengthen him upon the bed of languishing: thou wilt make all his bed in his sickness."

I speak peace over my child/children. The word of God says, "Great peace have they which love thy law, and nothing shall offend them" Psalm 119:165. Father, You promise to keep my children in perfect peace as long as they keep their minds on You, Isaiah 26:3. Therefore, Heavenly Father, I seal this prayer with Your word that says whatever we desire when we pray, we must believe that we have received it and shall have it in the name of Jesus Christ of Nazareth!

PRAYER FOR HUSBANDS

Heavenly Father, I come before You with a grateful heart. I stand in Your presence with a spirit of humility, just to say thank You for my husband. Lord, You have truly directed my path and I am certain that this is the person You appointed for me before the foundation of the world, Ephesians 1:3-4.

Father, You have commanded my husband to love me as You have loved the church and given Your life for it. It is my prayer that You amplify the love and compassion in him that could only come from You. I pray that his words will always match his actions and that he would be a man who always puts his family first. Lord, You have also said in Your word that my husband should leave mother and father and cleave to me, his wife, Genesis 2:24. Well, Lord, it is my prayer that I would be the kind of helpmeet to my husband that would make him always love me and have no desire for any other woman but me.

Father, I pray for faithfulness in my husband. You said that a faithful man shall abound with blessings, Proverbs 28:20. So, Lord, I cover my husband with Your grace and favour that will preserve his faithfulness, producing many blessings for our family.

PRAYER FOR HUSBANDS

I thank You, Lord, that my husband is a prudent man. Your word says, "A prudent man foresees the evil ahead and prepares himself," Proverbs 22:3.

Please continue to enable my husband to see ahead so that he can make wise decisions that will benefit our family. It is my prayer that You provide my husband with wisdom regarding our finances. Your word says, "My God shall supply all my needs according to His riches in glory in Christ Jesus," Philippians 4:19. So, as You provide for our needs, I decree and declare that my husband will be an excellent manager of our resources. I declare that my husband is a man of integrity, particularly in our marriage. Father, enable me to satisfy my husband in every area, causing him to only find comfort, peace, joy, and endless love with me, his helpmeet.

Lord, Your word says, "No temptation has overtaken a person except what is common to man. And God is faithful, that he will not let You be tempted beyond what You can bear. But when you are tempted, he will also provide a way of escape," 1 Corinthians 10:13. Lord, reinforce my husband's ability to resist temptation and remain faithful to our marriage.

PRAYER FOR HUSBANDS

I pray for patience and understanding in my husband. I pray that his patience and understanding would cause us to resolve all conflict amicably and seek ways to better our relationship.

Finally, Father, if there is any pride, arrogance, selfishness, greed, or dishonesty in him, I request that You remove it. I am reminding You of Your word that says, "Every plant not planted by You will be uprooted," Matthew 15:13. So, Lord, uproot out of my husband whatever You did not intend to be in him, in the name of Jesus Christ of Nazareth.

PRAYER FOR WIVES

Father God, thank You for this precious gift You gave me in the person of my wife. Father, I cover her with Your precious blood and with the authorized covering You gave me to cover her with. Lord, You have commanded me to be the head of my wife as You are the head of the Church (Ephesians 5:23). Teach me to lead my wife as well as my family in humility, compassion, faithfulness, and, more importantly, love. I pray that my wife and I would submit to each other, as You have commanded in Ephesians 5:21.

Heavenly Father, You have stated in Your word that while a person could inherit houses and riches, a prudent wife can only come from You (Proverbs 19:14). I decree and declare that I have a good, faithful, prudent, loyal, committed, and wise wife. As the Priest of our home and the head of my wife, I speak life over her. I declare that she will have excellent health, humility, grace, honor, patience, confidence, courage, and foresight. I declare that my wife exceeds that of a Proverbs 31 woman.

Lord, I pray for a spirit of excellence between us that will create a perpetual synergy between my wife and me. I pray that whatever we put our minds and hands to according to Your will shall prosper.

PRAYER FOR WIVES

According to Your law of unity, it is my prayer that my wife and I will always be on one accord, speaking the same language of unity, and as a result, nothing will be restrained from us (Genesis 11:6).Lord, I stand in complete agreement with Your word that says, "Let her be as the loving hind and pleasant roe. Let her breast always satisfy thee, and be thou ravished always with her love" (Proverbs 5:19). I pray for an impenetrable hedge to surround our union and that there will be no violation of our marriage.

I pray for great success for my wife and that she will be the head and not the tail, above only and not beneath (Deuteronomy 28:13). I command all generational curses, especially sickness, to be destroyed now. Sickness and disease shall never be her portion, in the mighty name of Jesus Christ of Nazareth.

Father God, because of my wife, I have received tremendous favour. I am certainly not surprised because Your word said, "He that finds a wife finds a good thing and obtains favour of the Lord" (Proverbs 18:22). Again, Lord, I thank You for this wonderful person You have blessed me within the person of my wife. I pray that we will grow old together even more committed than we are now in the name of Jesus Christ of Nazareth.

PRAYERS AGAINST CONFLICT IN MARRIAGES

Father, in the name of Your son Jesus Christ, you have stated in Your Word that Satan is the accuser of the brethren. You have also identified Satan as the thief who only shows up to kill, steal, and destroy (Revelation 12:10 and John 10:10). Most gracious Father, I present my marriage before You this day. Not only do I seek Your wisdom, but also Your knowledge and understanding to navigate Your will for our marriage. I cover our union with the whole armor of God as well as with the shed blood of Jesus Christ.

We are standing on Your Word concerning our marriage, "What God has joined together let no man separate" (Mark 10:9). Father, I am also in search of favour for our marriage. Again, Your Word states that he who finds a wife finds a good thing and shall obtain favour of the Lord. Lord, if there is ever a time we need Your promised favour, it is now.

Every spirit of division, discord, and divorce, I cancel and bind Your evil powers against the divine purpose of my marriage. Every spirit that is on assignment to disrupt the synergy in my marriage, I declare confusion upon that spirit in the name of Jesus Christ.

PRAYER AGAINST CONFLICT IN MARRIAGE

Every spirit that is on assignment to disrupt the synergy in my marriage, I declare confusion upon that spirit in the name of Jesus Christ.

I command every spirit of dishonesty, lust, fornication, adultery, and mismanagement of our marital resources to leave our God-ordained union by the authority of Jesus Christ. Every manipulative, controlling, and anti-leadership spirit challenging the leadership of my marital covenant, and particularly the leadership of our marital union, I command You to cease and desist now!

By the authority of the Lord Jesus Christ, I decree and declare that every spirit opposing our marriage be tormented before its time and cast into the abyss in the name of Jesus Christ. Every witchcraft spirit of frustration and foolish disagreements, I render You powerless in the name of Jesus Christ. I command every love spell, every spirit spouse, every hex, along with every evil altar speaking against the destiny of our covenant marital union, to be cast down by the blood of Jesus Christ of Nazareth. It was and still is God's original intent that no man separates our covenant union.

PRAYER AGAINST CONFLICT IN MARRIAGE

Therefore, I declare and decree to the powers of darkness in the spiritual as well as physical realm the cancellation of all untimely death, accidents, depression, confusion, fear, anxiety, and sexual violations that You intend to introduce to our marital covenant. I silence every evil gossiping voice of negativity and declare null and void every evil sacrifice against our marital covenant.

Heavenly Father, Your Word says in 1 Peter 4:8, "Above all, love each other deeply, because love covers a multitude of sins." Lord, not only do we receive this over our marriage, but we also bind our faith to this with the commitment to live this in the name of Jesus Christ.

We are again reminded of Your Word that says, "So they are no longer two but one flesh. What God has joined together, let no man put asunder" (Matthew 19:6).

Father, I pray that we would move in unity, speaking with one voice and being on one accord. According to Your law of unity, nothing will be withheld from us (Genesis 11:6). I pray for a spirit of submission in our union. You have commanded us to submit one to another in the fear of the Lord (Ephesians 5:2).

PRAYER AGAINST CONFLICT IN MARRIAGE

I command every soul tie to be dissolved along with all spiritual marriages that may have entered our union via our dreams or former sexual partners before our marriage. We cast down all imagination and everything that exalts itself above the knowledge of God, bringing into captivity every thought to the obedience of Christ (2 Corinthians 10:5).

Now, Lord, we declare peace over our marriage, that peace that only You can give, which passes all understanding, in the name of Jesus Christ of Nazareth!

PRAYING THE WORD OF GOD AGAINST INVISIBLE FORCES OPERATING AGAINST ME AND MY FAMILY

Heavenly Father in the name of Your Son Jesus Christ we command that our names be removed from every evil register, every evil altar, and every evil ordinance that has been spiritually written against us. Lord, every altar operating against our destiny, we demand that those evil altars, the evil conditions and terms that were made against us be destroyed by Holy Ghost fire in the name of Jesus Christ!

Lord, let Your fire dissolve every ancestral curse such as anti-marriage, anti-success, anti-progress, poverty, rejection, sickness, and disgrace. Let all ancestral curses never be reconciled again in our lives in the mighty name of Jesus Christ!

Father Your word says in Lamentations 5:7 that, "Our ancestors have sinned, and now they are dead, but we the current generation are left to bear their iniquities."

Lord, we speak Your word against the above spiritual law and because of Your finished work on the cross we bind ourselves to Your covenant law that supersedes the above law and that law states,

"Christ has redeemed us from the curse of the law, being made a curse for us." For it is written in Galatians 3:14-15, "Cursed is everyone that hangs on a tree, that the blessings of Abraham might come to the Gentiles through Jesus Christ; that we might receive the promise of the Spirit through faith." We abandon the curse and receive the Abrahamic blessings in the name of Jesus Christ.

Father God, not only do we believe in Your finished works on the cross, we also believe that as a result of Your finished work You have quickened us together with You. For You have forgiven us of all our trespasses along with blotting out the handwriting of ordinances that was against us, which was contrary to us, and took it out of the way, nailing it to the cross according to Colossians 2:13-14.

Father, based on Your new covenant and the spiritual laws that accompany it, we silence every evil voice speaking against our destinies. We bring into captivity all bad thoughts that have created patterns of negativity in our lives via generational curses according to Your word in Second Corinthians 10:5.

We break all cycles of defeat, depression, failure, hijacked destinies, poverty, divorce, lack of knowledge, lack of wisdom, lack of understanding and lack of the fear of the Lord in the mighty name of Jesus Christ. Amen.

PRAYER FOR RELEASE OF GENERATIONAL BLESSINGS

Father God, firstly, I thank You for divine knowledge. According to Your word in Hosea 4:6 and Isaiah 5:13, You will prevent us from being destroyed or held captive. Lord, I am asking You on this day and in the days to come to "RELEASE" and cause to fall upon me as well as my bloodline at the appointed times all generational blessings of our forefathers that came about as a result of their obedience of honoring Your statues, commandments, and covenants.

Lord, please let those generational blessings come alive and speak to the troubles and snares that have been embedded in our destinies designed to hinder us. Lord, remember the commitment and prayers that our ancestors prayed to You concerning our current generation. Heavenly Father, cause their words not to fall to the ground in the name of Your Son Jesus Christ. Father, Your word, which is spiritual law, says in Lamentations 5:7, "Our ancestors sinned and have died, and we are left to bear their punishment." Father, while I am convinced that this is Your law for generational curses, I am also convinced that the opposite is also true.

PRAYER FOR RELEASE OF GENERATIONAL BLESSINGS

Our ancestors have also obeyed, honored Your laws and covenants and they are now dead. However, we that are alive will receive of the blessings they have left in place in the mighty and matchless name of Your Son and my Savior Jesus Christ. Amen!

PRAYERS
FOR
SPIRITUAL
WARFARE

SENDING THE FIRE OF GOD

There are two scriptures that characterize God as a consuming fire, Deuteronomy 4:24 and Hebrews 12:29. Why don't you intensify your prayers today, by sending the fire of God at the root of those relentless and stubborn issues in your life?

Heavenly Father, I accept the word that describes You as a consuming fire. I know that even though that fire can be used for refining and purifying, this is not the use for which I approach Your throne today. Instead, Father, it is my prayer that You send spiritual fire to the spiritual root of the constant and stubborn problems, that have become yokes and burdens in my life. Father, whatever has kept me from where I should have been at this point in my life, please release me into Your intended path for my life.

Lord, I pray that Your fire would consume and annihilate all evidence of the spiritual forces working against me, in the mighty name of Your Son Jesus Christ. Father, I pray for the destruction of all evil forces in my life. Father, readjust my way of thinking so that once I have been spiritually set free from the devices of the enemy, I will not continue to be in bondage in my mind.

SENDING THE FIRE OF GOD

Lord, send Your angels to war against the powers of darkness. Bring their plans and devices to failure. Disgrace all the powers of darkness working against me. Let not the enemy prevail against me. Let me always be aware that You are the Chief-in-Command with all wars waged against my life.

Father, I stand today on Your word that says in Mark 11:24-26, whatsoever things I desire when I pray, I must believe that I have received them and I shall have them in the matchless name of Your Son Jesus Christ. Amen.

LET THE FORCES OF DARKNESS BE DISABLED BY HOLY GHOST FIRE

Heavenly Father, I speak to every "spiritual leader" or enemy speaking against my God ordained destiny, that their deep-seated hateful and harmful words fall to the ground in the name of Jesus Christ! Let every agent of Satan manipulating my prosperity, my relationships, my marriage, my health, and my mental state be destroyed by the invisible fire of God in the name of Jesus Christ!

Let every boss, supervisor, manager or whomever is sitting on my promotion, increase, or advancement be arrested and judged by the Spirit of the living God in the name of Jesus Christ! I command all demonic spirits of mental torment that have been targeted against my mind that are maintaining the cycles of frustration, anger, fatigue, discouragement, confusion, and depression to be unseated right now by the presence and fire of the true living God in the name of His Son Jesus Christ!

Whatever has been spiritually planted on my property, secretly placed in my home, and covertly put in my food, to spiritually manipulate my health, I pray that God Almighty will destroy all demonic spiritual sources and bring its agents to shame and to openly disgrace each of them in the name of Jesus Christ!

Every false prophet, apostle, evangelist, pastor, teacher and all agents of Satan, or whomever has disguised themselves as true men and women of God be publicly exposed for who they really are in the name of Jesus Christ.

I further pray by the power of the Holy Spirit that every evil covenant that has been established by these shameless evil charlatans via the receiving of my money {seed}, evil miracle cloths, demonic "holy water," the laying on of demonic hands, demonic spiritual baths, or any other form of evil acts; I ask Lord, let these evil spiritual covenants knowingly or unknowingly done to me or any other victims be destroyed by Your everlasting all-consuming fire in the name of Your Son Jesus Christ!

Let every false prophecy that was spoken over my life that in reality delayed my life be broken by the shed blood of Jesus Christ! I command every generational curse to be permanently disabled and destroyed by the authority of my Lord and Savior Jesus Christ!

LET THE FORCES OF DARKNESS BE DISABLED

Finally, as a result of God answering the above prayers and supplications, I now decree and declare Joel 2:25 that says, "And I will restore to you the years that the locust hath eaten, the cankerworm, and the caterpillar, and the palmerworm, my great army which I sent among you." And over every life that comes in agreement with this prayer, I decree it in the name of Jesus Christ. Amen!

PRAYER AGAINST SPIRITUAL ROBBERS

Father God, in the name of Your only begotten Son Jesus Christ, I come before Your throne of grace and mercy seeking Your divine help. Lord, I come reminding You of Your word that says, "I can do all things through Christ that strengthens me," according to Your word in Philippians 4:13. Heavenly Father, with Your divine assistance I command every spiritual robber to be paralyzed by the power and authority of Your word that says, "That at the name of Jesus every knee shall bow of things in heaven (the spiritual realm) and things in earth, and things under the earth," according to Philippians 2:10.

Lord, I decree and declare that not only have I discovered and identified these spiritual robbers in my dreams stealing from me, but by the authority of Your word, I command these same spiritual robbers to return and restore unto me seven fold of what they have originally taken from me, including the wealth of this house according to Your word in Proverbs 6:31. Father God, just how You have empowered the right hand of King Cyrus and You went before him leveling the obstacles that were in his way while at the same time providing him with the hidden treasures as well as the hidden riches of secret places according to Your word in Isaiah 45:1-3.

PRAYER AGAINST SPIRITUAL ROBBERS

Lord, I am asking You to visit my life with the same favour extended to King Cyrus in the name of Your Son Jesus Christ.

Finally, Lord, You said in Your word that all things are possible to him that believes according to Mark 9:23. Therefore, Father, I believe Your word. I believe that every spiritual robber has been subdued spiritually and they are all under my feet. I further seal these spiritual robbers' fate by commanding them to be tormented before their time according to Matthew 8:29 in the mighty name of Jesus Christ. Amen.

PRAYER AGAINST EVIL ALTARS

I render every aggressive altar impotent in the mighty name of Jesus. Every evil altar erected against me, be disgraced in the name of Jesus. Anything done against me under a demonic anointing, be nullified in the name of Jesus. I curse every local altar fashioned against me in the name of Jesus. Let the hammer of the Almighty God, smash every evil altar erected against me in the name of Jesus. O Lord, send Your fire to destroy every evil altar fashioned against me in the name of Jesus.

Every evil priest ministering against me at the evil altar, receive Holy Ghost fire in the name of Jesus. Let the word of God be your portion. God's promises to me are, I will curse those that curse you, and I will bless those that bless you (Genesis 12:3). Let every satanic priest ministering against me at any evil altar be confronted by the Angels of the Lord in the name of Jesus. Father, I thank You that You have blessed me with all spiritual blessings in heavenly places according to Ephesians 1:3. Let every curse sent at me from the evil priest be turned into a blessing.

Father, I am convinced that because all things are possible to those that believe, I know that my name and all that concerns me have been erased from all evil altars and all evil covenants in the name of Jesus Christ.

PRAYER AGAINST THE SPIRIT OF DELAY

Heavenly Father, I come in agreement with Your word according to Jeremiah 23:29 which says, "Is not my word like a fire? saith the Lord; and like a hammer that breaketh the rock in pieces?" I speak this word with the authority You've given me and release Your judgment, like You did in the day of Sodom and Gomorrah. Father, every plan, plot, scheme, distraction, manipulation, seen and unseen launched by these spirits, I command its spiritual and physical counsel to fall to the ground in the mighty name of Jesus Christ!

Heavenly Father, I command this evil spirit of delay by the power of Your word and the blood of Your Son Jesus Christ to release and restore all that he has stolen from me and Your people. I command all spiritual and physical counsel against me to fall to the ground, only to become stepping stones to my elevation in the mighty name of Jesus. I bind myself to Your promise that said, You would restore unto me the years that the enemy has stolen (Joel 2:25).

I COMMAND THIS THIEF "THE SPIRIT OF DELAY" TO RESTORE SEVENFOLD ALL THAT HE HAS STOLEN INCLUDING THE SUBSTANCE OF HIS HOUSE ACCORDING TO THE WORD OF GOD IN THE NAME OF JESUS CHRIST! AMEN.

THE GREAT PHAROH WILL FALL

I command every Pharaoh working against my destiny to fall and fail now in the mighty name of Jesus Christ! Anyone or anything that has hindered me from where I should have been at this stage of my life according to the will of God and His chosen purpose for my life, God commanded Moses to say to Pharaoh, "let My people go" (Exodus 7:16 and Exodus 9:11). Therefore, I command the realm of the spirit to give up all my spiritual blessings that have been stolen from me, in the mighty name of Jesus Christ!

Every evil sacrifice of my forefathers, all evil voices of witchcraft speaking from every evil altar against my destiny that has paralyzed my prosperity, I command those evil sacrifices and evil voices, along with every evil altar to be silenced and destroyed by the fire of the Holy Ghost in the mighty name of Jesus Christ! Amen.

DEFEATING THE ENEMY WITH THE WORD

Heavenly Father, I outfit myself and all that concerns me with the whole armor of God today, which You said in Your word will cause us to stand against the wiles of the Devil according to Ephesians 6:11-13. I declare the blood of Jesus Christ against all evil voices speaking against my destiny. I command by the authority and power of God that those evil voices will be silenced, brought to shame, disgraced, and that their despicable vile counsels will fall to the ground in the name of Jesus Christ!

Spirit of disgrace, I speak and declare disgrace to you in the mighty name of Jesus Christ! Father, those that are relentless and have no respect for Your anointed or insist on projecting curses and slander, well, I stand on Your word that says we must love our enemies and bless them that curse us, and do good to them that hate us, and pray for them which despitefully use and persecute us that we may be the children of our Father which is in heaven (Matthew 5:44-45).

DEFEATING THE ENEMY WITH THE WORD

Heavenly Father, dissolve by Your fire every witchcraft altar that has been erected against my destiny and the destinies of my family members as well as our health, prosperity, promotion, and all that You have made available to us in the name of Your Son Jesus Christ!

Father, I command the spirits of delay and setbacks that have been assigned to me and Your people be disabled indefinitely by the power of Your word that says, no weapon formed against us shall prosper and any tongue that rises up against us, we condemn it in the mighty name of Jesus Christ according to Isaiah 54:17.

Lord, I speak to the spirits of weariness, frustration, procrastination, hurt, defeat, failure, and most of all unforgiveness that have been ruling me and the lives of my family members. I command them to be destroyed by Your word as written in Jeremiah 23:29, "Is not my word like as a fire? saith the Lord; and like a hammer that breaketh the rock in pieces?" It is this word Heavenly Father that I stand on while declaring and decreeing against the forces of evil that are always rioting against my destiny and the destiny of my family in the name of Jesus Christ.

DEFEATING THE ENEMY WITH THE WORD

Finally, Father, Your word says in Ecclesiastes 5:12, "The sleep of a laboring man is sweet." Therefore, by the power and authority of Christ Jesus, I subdue all spirits of insomnia, restlessness, fatigue, nervousness, and all associating spirits. I receive and covenant with Your word that says in Psalm 127:2, "for so he giveth his beloved sleep." Therefore, I accept and believe Your word in the name of Your Son Jesus Christ. Amen!

PRAYER FOR DIVINE ARMOR AND PROTECTION

This day I equip myself with the whole armor of God, according to the constitution of the spiritual and physical realm. I am strongly advised to do so, that I may be able to stand against the wiles of the devil, and to stand in the evil day, Ephesians 6:11, 13. Therefore, by faith, I now equip my spiritual and physical being with the helmet of salvation. I stand, girding my waist with truth and equipping myself with the breastplate of righteousness. I armor my feet with the preparation of the gospel of peace. I now take up the shield of faith, so that I may be able to quench the fiery darts of the wicked. Finally, I take possession of the sword of the Spirit, which is the word of God.

Father, You promised in Your word, according to Psalm 91:11-12, that You have given Your angels charge over me to keep me in all my ways. Lord, You said that Your detailed security assigned angelic protection will bear me up in their hands if I as much as dash my foot against a stone. Father, I remind You of Your word regarding my spiritual protection. You said, "To which of the angels did You say at any time, 'Sit on my right hand, until I make Your enemies Your footstool?'

PRAYER FOR DIVINE ARMOR AND PROTECTION

Are they not all ministering spirits, sent forth to minister for them who shall be heirs of salvation?" Hebrews 1:13-14. I receive Your word and Your promises of help and protection. I will speak and declare Your goodness and mercies.

I submit to Your will and divine timing, and I ask You to catapult me into the destiny You had originally ordained for me. Though I walk through the valley of the shadow of death, I will fear no evil. For You are with me, Your rod and Your staff they comfort me.

You, O Lord, have prepared a table before me in the presence of my enemies. You, O Lord, have anointed my head with oil. My cup overflows. Surely goodness and mercy shall follow me all the days of my life, and I will dwell in the house of the Lord forever, in the name of Jesus Christ of Nazareth. Psalm 23:3-6.

TERMINATING EVIL COVENANTS

Once again, Heavenly Father, I repent of all my sins and cover myself with the whole armor of God and the blood of Jesus Christ. Father, when I accepted the free gift of salvation, at that moment, a covenant was established between You and me. That covenant has not only reconciled me back to God the Father, but it has also made me the righteousness of God in Christ Jesus.

I now renounce, denounce, dismiss, reject, and divorce myself from all evil covenants I have established with all evil entities, whether they be spiritual or physical covenants. I divorce myself from all secret societies, Freemasonry, Eastern Star, fraternities, sororities, and any organization where I made a written, verbal, or even blood oath, pledge, contract, agreement, or covenant. By the shed blood of Jesus Christ, I command every evil spirit at those evil altars that I once served, knowingly or unknowingly, to release its evil hold on my destiny, health, wealth, children, and all that I have foolishly surrendered to those altars in the name of Jesus Christ.

I declare that my Savior and Lord Jesus Christ blotted out the handwriting of ordinance that was against me, which was contrary to my destiny. He took it out of the way, nailing it to the cross, Colossians 2:13.

TERMINATING EVIL COVENANTS

Lord, please forgive me for any evil ritual I have performed. Forgive me for every evil ceremony I engaged in. I beg Your forgiveness for every spiritual bath, every incision, and every marking on my body and skin that was a part of my initiation or points of contact for evil spirits. I divorce myself from these evils and renounce all my participation in these evil events.

Lord, I am ashamed to know I served other gods, ignorantly invoking generational curses into my bloodline, Exodus 20:3-5. Father, now that I am a repairer of the breach and the restorer of paths to dwell in as a result of the fasting protocols of Isaiah 58, I pray that You rain down spiritual fire and brimstone against my evil works, as You did in the time of Sodom and Gomorrah. I decree and declare that the generational curses cease and desist and become null and void in the name of Jesus Christ. I command every spiritual activation of untimely death, poverty, stagnation, anti-progress, confusion, depression, anxiety attack, relationship issues, divorce, barrenness, and rejection to cease.

I decree and declare, "If God be for me, who can be against me?" Romans 8:31. I decree and declare, "Who shall separate me from the love of Christ? Shall tribulation, or distress, persecution or famine, nakedness, peril or sword?

TERMINATING EVIL COVENANTS

As it is written, for thy sake we are killed all day long, we are accounted as sheep for the slaughter. However, in all things, we are more than conquerors through Him that loved us," Romans 8:35-37.

I decree to every evil altar, every evil voice, and every evil sacrifice that I once gave myself to or demonic rituals and pledges I once participated in. I rededicate my body, spirit, and soul as a living sacrifice, holy and acceptable unto God, which is my reasonable service. I refuse to be conformed to this world. Instead, I insist on being transformed by the renewing of my mind so that I will be able to identify and prove what is that good, acceptable, and perfect will of God, Romans 12:1-2.

Father God, I now bind myself to Your promises that came through the covenant I have with You. You said, "Therefore, if any man is in Christ, he is a new creature; old things have passed away; behold, all things have become new" (2 Corinthians 5:17).

Lord, because of the new covenant I have with You, I command every evil spirit with whom I had previous covenants, which enabled them to rob me of my spiritual blessings, to depart from me.

TERMINATING EVIL COVENANTS

I command, by the authority of Jesus Christ, that they return to me everything they have stolen sevenfold, in the name of Jesus Christ (Proverbs 6:30-31). Lord, You promise that the righteous shall be recompensed on the earth (Proverbs 11:31a). Father, as a righteous person, I qualify to be repaid for all the losses I have suffered under the oppressive and deceitful hand of the kingdom of darkness. The God of Abraham, Isaac, and Jacob, I receive Your promise that says, "I will restore to you the years that the locust has eaten, the cankerworm, the caterpillar, and the palmerworm" (Joel 2:25).

Finally, Father, let Your peace that surpasses all understanding descend upon me. Keep my mind sound, remove all fears, for You did not give me a spirit of fear but of power, love, and a sound mind. I forgive everyone who has wronged me, and I apologize from my heart for all the wrongs I have done to others in the name of Jesus Christ of Nazareth.

MISCELLANEOUS PRAYERS

PRAYER FOR HEALING

Father, I thank You for Your Son, Jesus Christ, whom You have given the authority to reconcile us back to You. I confess my sins before You, Lord, and ask for forgiveness and mercy in the name of Your Son Jesus Christ.

Today, Lord, I come before You seeking healing and deliverance from the spirit of infirmity. I know that true healing comes through Your Son Jesus Christ. In fact, You said that Jesus was wounded for our transgressions, He was bruised for our iniquity. The chastisement for our peace was upon Him, and by His stripes, we are healed (Isaiah 53:5). Lord, I claim what Jesus has done for me and everyone who believes. I believe that I am healed of all sickness and disease because of the stripes Jesus bore for me.

In the beginning was the Word, and the Word was with God, and the Word was God. You further stated that the Word was made flesh and dwelt among us (John 1:1, 14). Father, I am aware that the Word made flesh was indeed Your Son Jesus Christ. Therefore, I understand when You said that You sent forth Your Word and healed them and delivered them from their destruction (Psalm 107:20). It is clear that the Word was Jesus Christ made flesh.

PRAYER FOR HEALING

Again, 1 John 5:7 says that there are three that bear record in Heaven: the Father, the Word (Jesus Christ), and the Holy Ghost. Revelation 19:13 says, "And He (Jesus Christ) was clothed with a vesture dipped in blood, and His name is called the Word of God.

Father God, not only am I convinced that Your Son and my Savior Jesus Christ is my healer, which is Your Word, but I also bind myself to Your Word as I declare scriptures of healing. The Word says, "According to my faith, be it unto me," and that I cannot please You without my faith (Matthew 9:29 and Hebrews 11:6).

I decree, declare, and engage the following spiritual laws of healing:

"He has sent His Word to heal me" (Psalm 107:20).

"He heals the brokenhearted and binds up their wounds" (Psalm 147:3).

"Because of His stripes, I am healed" (Isaiah 53:5).

"Healing is the children's bread" (Matthew 15:26).

"The Lord will sustain me on my sick bed, during my illness, He will restore me to full health" (Psalm 41:3).

"Heal me, O Lord, and I shall be healed" (Jeremiah 17:14).

PRAYER FOR HEALING

"Confess your faults one to another, and pray one for another, that you may be healed. The effectual fervent prayer of a righteous avails much" (James 5:14-16).

"For I will restore health unto thee, and I will heal thee of thy wounds, says the Lord" (Jeremiah 30:17).

"And you shall serve the Lord thy God, and He shall bless thy bread and thy water, and I will take away sickness away from the midst of thee" (Exodus 23:25).

"Bless the Lord, O my soul, and do not forget His benefits, who forgives all iniquities, who heals all your diseases" (Psalm 103:2-3).

"O Lord, by these things, men live, and in all these is the life of my spirit. Restore me to health and let me live" (Isaiah 38:16).

"A merry heart does good like medicine" (Proverbs 17:22).

So, Father, I claim, believe, and receive these promises in the name of Jesus Christ. Your Word says, "All things are possible to those who believe" (Mark 9:23).

PRAYER FOR HEALING

"My son, give attention to my words; incline your ears to my sayings. Do not let them depart from your eyes; keep them in the midst of your heart. For they are life to those who find them and health to all their flesh" (Proverbs 4:20-22).

"He gives power to the weak, and to those who have no might He increases their strength. Those who wait on the Lord shall renew their strength. They shall mount up with wings like eagles, they shall run and not be weary, they shall walk and not faint" (Isaiah 40:29-31).

PRAYER FOR SINGLES

Heavenly Father, I come before You once again seeking Your favour and grace. Thank You for the open-door policy that allows me to approach Your throne at any time. Lord, Your word says, "If we hide our sins, we shall not prosper," Proverbs 28:13a. At this point, Father, I am laying it out on the table, and I confess and repent of all violations I have committed against Your laws. I believe by faith that not only have You forgiven me, but You have also tossed my sins into the sea of forgetfulness.

According to Genesis 2:18, You have made it clear that it is not beneficial for us to be alone. You also mentioned in Ecclesiastes 4:9, "Two are better than one because they will have a good reward for their labor. Lord, I bind my faith to Your infallible word, asking You to direct me to the person that You had appointed for me before the foundation of the world, according to Ephesians 1:3-4.

Help me to prepare myself for Your best. Assist me in not being conformed to this world. Instead, I want to be transformed by the renewing of my mind so that I can now prove and identify who is that good and acceptable person You have reserved just for me, Romans 12:2.

PRAYER FOR SINGLES

I have made the decision to follow Your protocol that will assure me that You will direct me in the right direction. You said that I must trust in You with all my heart, lean not unto my own understanding, and in all my ways, I must acknowledge You, and now You will direct my path, Proverbs 3:5-6.

By faith, I receive Your promise to lead me to Your best for my life. "I will instruct thee and teach thee in the way which thou shall go, and I will guide thee with mine eyes", Psalm 32:8. Lord, as You sent an angel ahead of Abraham's servant to secure a life partner for Abraham's son Isaac, Genesis 24:7, please do likewise for me.

Heavenly Father, I am confident that You have heard me, and I seal this prayer by standing on Your word that says, "And this is the confidence that we have in him, that, if we ask anything according to His will, he heard us. If we know that he heard us, whatsoever we ask, we know that we have the petition that we desire of him in the name of Jesus Christ," 1 John 5:14-15.

PRAYER FOR THE WORKPLACE

Father, today as I prepare for work, I want to thank You not only for the gift of life but also for blessing me with employment to assist in meeting my needs. Lord, due to the spiritual hostility at my workplace, I am outfitting myself with the whole armor of God so that I can stand against the wiles of the devil, according to Ephesians 6:12.

Father, You said to Your servant Joshua, "Every place that the sole of your foot shall tread upon, that have I given you," Joshua 1:3. Lord, please favour me in my workplace by giving me power over every opposing spirit at my place of employment, such as spirits of witchcraft, controlling spirits, narcissistic spirits, deceitful, hateful, unforgiving, and vindictive spirits, as well as spirits of oppression, delay, stagnation, and anti-progress.

Heavenly Father, based on the knowledge of Your word, I am fully aware that my fight is not with the people at my workplace. Instead, my fight is against the evil spiritual hierarchy of the kingdom of darkness, such as principalities, powers, rulers of the darkness of this world, and spiritual wickedness in high places, Ephesians 6:12.

PRAYER FOR THE WORKPLACE

So, I am grateful for my spiritual reinforcement that You have provided me, such as Your angels whom You have given charge over me to keep me in all my ways, so that if I as much as dash my foot against a stone, they are commanded by You to gather me in their hands, Psalm 91:11-12. Lord, help me not to envy those whom the spirit of oppression is using to oppress me, and help me not to choose any of their ways, Proverbs 3:31. Even though I know I am in a spiritually toxic environment, I stand on Your word that assures me that while the curse of the Lord is in the house (workplace) of the wicked, You also bless the habitation of the just, Proverbs 3:33.

Lord, I take authority over the spirits of dishonesty, crookedness, evil compromise, as well as all evil enterprises set up against myself and all those who are covered under the blood of Jesus Christ in my workplace. I have made the decision to follow Your command, as hard as it may be, to bless those who have and are cursing me, and to pray for those who mistreat me and say all manner of things against me, Luke 6:28. You command that I must not rejoice when my enemy falls and let not my heart be glad when they stumble, lest the Lord see it and it displeases Him, and He turns away his wrath from him (my enemy), Proverbs 24:17-18.

PRAYER FOR THE WORKPLACE

I truly want to do things the way You prescribe them to be done, simply because I want a God-intended result. Lord, I pray for the souls that are lost in this place and have become consumed by the spirits of greed, pride, arrogance, and control. I pray for their salvation as well as their release from the invisible forces that they are unaware of controlling them. You said, it is not Your desire that anyone should perish but everyone should repent 2 Peter 3:9.

Finally, Father, I pray that You reinforce my spiritual hedge of protection around myself and those who place their trust in You, as You did for Your servant Job, Job 1:10. I ask these things in the name of Your Son and our Savior, Jesus Christ of Nazareth.

ABOUT THE AUTHOR

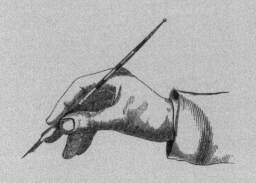

KEVIN L. A. EWING

Pastor Kevin L.A. Ewing is well-known throughout the beautiful islands of the Bahamas and the world for his dynamic, prolific, and detailed teachings on the word of God. For many years, he has published religious articles in the Freeport News and Tribune Newspaper in the Bahamas. He has partnered with local and international ministries through radio talk shows, conferences, workshops, training seminars, revivals, and small group meetings to help build, structure, and equip them with his teachings on spiritual warfare and dream interpretation. He is also the administrator, producer, and writer for his blog site, "Journey into God's Word," and his weekly radio show, "The Kevin L. A. Ewing Spiritual Insight Show," which airs on DOVE 103.7 FM every Saturday.

Pastor Ewing believes that the spirit world is the parent world of our natural world and that whatever transpires in the spirit world is continuously seeking permission to manifest its will in our natural world. He is further convinced that God has equipped every human being with the tools to dream, where spiritual monitors peer into the spirit realm, revealing excerpts of what's pending in the spiritual world for their lives or the lives of others. It's this aspect of his ministry on which he thrives.

KEVIN L. A. EWING

Pastor Ewing is a profound and detailed teacher who dissects the word of God in a way that even a child can understand. His teachings are littered with scriptures, and he believes that the scriptures are the spiritual laws and principles that govern the spirit and the physical realm. His most noted scripture, which describes the foundation of his ministry, is Hosea 4:6, "the people of God are destroyed for lack of knowledge." (Proverbs 11:9b "But through knowledge shall the just be delivered.") He believes that the lack of knowledge as it relates to spiritual laws and principles continuously determines failure or success for the believers of Jesus Christ.

Pastor Ewing is married to the lovely Mrs. Dedre Ewing. He is the proud father of his beautiful children Chavez, Garrett, Kevin, Kia, and Kristina.

For More Information Please Visit:
www.kevinlaewing.com

RECOMMEDNED BOOKS

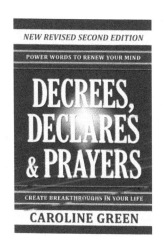 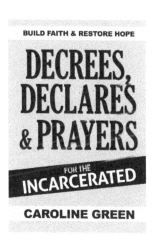

AVAILBLE ON
WWW.IAMCAROLINEGREEN.COM

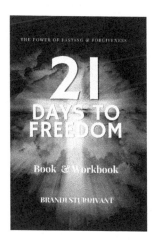 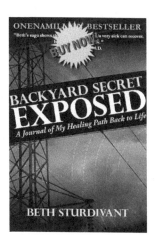

AVAILBLE ON
WWW.IAMBRANDIMARIE.COM

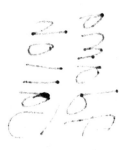

Adama
Jalloh